C000057351

PLAGUE AND DISEASE

RICHARD WORSNOP

GENERAL EDITOR: DAVID PENROSE

Great Horwood C. of E. Combined
School, Great Horwood, Milton
Keynes, MK17 0RG

8004691

COLLINS
EDUCATIONAL

INTRODUCTION

Plague and Disease will stimulate children to gain a real insight into the danger-filled lives of people who lived in the poor housing and bad sanitary conditions of the past. The book helps to develop history skills but will also be useful in modern health education studies.

Through documentary and photographic evidence children will learn to evaluate, deduce and compare. The great killer diseases of the past – plague, cholera and tuberculosis are described, together with their effects on humankind and the fear and superstition they inspired. The book traces the long fight against disease and ignorance and shows the importance today of the lessons learnt in the past.

Richard Worsnop is the Head of a Junior school in Kirklees, West Yorkshire and has had teaching experience in Hull, Halifax, Rotherham and Barnsley.

© Richard Worsnop 1987

First published in Great Britain 1987 by
Collins Educational
8 Grafton Street, London W1X 3LA

Reprinted 1988

Typeset by V & M Graphics Ltd, Aylesbury, Bucks.
Printed in Great Britain by Martin's of Berwick

ISBN 0 00 315412 2

All rights reserved. No part of this publication may be reproduced, stored in a retrieval system, or transmitted, in any form or by any means, electronic, mechanical, photocopying, recording or otherwise, without the prior permission of the publishers.

CONTENTS

TABLE 1

Incubation and Exclusion Periods of the Commoner Communicable Diseases

Disease	Normal Incubation Period (in days)	Period of communicability	Minimal Period of Exclusion	
			Cases (subject to clinical recovery)	Contacts
Chickenpox	11–21	From 1 day before to 6 days after appearance of rash	6 days from onset of rash	None
Diptheria	2–5	Whilst the organism is present in nose or throat	Until bacterio-logical examination is clear	Until bacterio-logical examination is clear
German Measles (Rubella)	14–21	From a few days before to 4 days after onset of rash	4 days from onset of rash	None
Measles	10–15 (commonly 10 to onset of illness and 14 to appearance of rash)	From a few days before to 5 days after onset of rash	7 days from onset of rash	None
Mumps	12–26 (commonly 18)	From a few days before onset of symptoms to subsidence of swelling	Until swelling has subsided	None
Smallpox	7–16 (commonly 12)	From first symptoms to disappearance of all scabs	Until declared free from infection by MOH (Medical Officer of Health)	16 days and until declared free from infection by MOH
Tuberculosis (Primary)	4–6 weeks	Whilst organism is present in sputum	Until declared non-infectious	None
Typhoid fever	7–21 (usually 14)	Whilst organism is present in stools or urine	Until bacterio-logical examination is clear	None except for home contacts
Paratyphoid fever	1–10			
Whooping cough (Pertussis)	7–10	From 7 days after exposure to 21 days after onset of paroxysmal cough	21 days from onset of paroxysmal cough	None

Health at home and at school

What happens when you are ill?

If you are very ill the doctor calls at your home to see you. If you are not too ill you go to see the doctor in the surgery. You may have to stay in bed. You may be given pills or medicines or ointments. The doctor may say you should have special food and drinks — glucose, for example. When you are beginning to get better you may be advised to get plenty of fresh air.

The doctor may say you should be kept away from other children during your illness. Some diseases are very *infectious*. This means they can easily be passed to other people. Can you think, for example, how you could avoid passing a nasty cold or cough to other people?

Opposite is part of an Infectious DiseasesList which schools have as a guide to some illnesses. You won't find coughs and colds on the list. Instead, you will find diseases which can be much more dangerous.

Can you explain the words incubation, communicability, exclusion, contacts? Look them up in a dictionary if you don't know what they mean.

Make a class or school graph to show how many children have suffered from these diseases:

Measles
German measles
Mumps
Chickenpox
Whooping cough
Typhus
Smallpox
Typhoid
Diphtheria

Look at your results. What do you notice? Are there any diseases which you had not heard of before? Does that tell you anything?

Compare your graph results with these figures from Huddersfield about 90 years ago:

Deaths in Huddersfield

	1901	1902	1903	1904
Scarlet Fever	6	11	15	10
Measles	13	58	0	75
Diphtheria	6	15	14	14
Whooping Cough	2	46	16	25
Typhoid	18	5	8	7
Diarrhoea	89	19	25	49
Smallpox	0	1	2	1

Make a block graph showing the deaths from each disease in the four years.

Which do you think was the worst disease? Have any of your class ever had it?

Which is the disease which caused the fewest deaths?

Can you see anything unusual about the deaths caused by measles?

All headteachers keep a diary or *log book* in which they write a record of what happens in schools. Here are three entries from a log book which was written a long time ago.

December 1888   Two pupils have typhoid.
January 1894   School closed because of diphtheria.
November 1899 Percy Spencer died from Scarlet Fever.

It would be very unusual to write anything like this today. Can you think why?

Many schools still have their old log books. Perhaps you could get permission to read some of your school's log books and search for any accounts of illnesses.

Finding a cure

During the last hundred years scientists have discovered cures for many diseases. They have also discovered causes of diseases, and this is probably even more important as we can now stop them starting and spreading.

Today there are many people helping us to keep healthy. Things have not always been like this.

When you visit your doctor's surgery you see posters on the walls. Perhaps there are booklets and leaflets for you to take away. These are all there to give people information, help and advice.

What sort of advice are these leaflets giving?

Can you tell which people they are intended for?

This is a photograph of a school nurse visiting a school in London in 1907. What do you think she is looking for?

Does the school nurse visit your school and look through the children's hair? If so, she will be looking for the nits or eggs of the head louse — just like the nurse in the old photograph.

For what other reasons do doctors and nurses visit your school? When were you last medically examined?

When doctors and nurses first began visiting schools about 90 years ago they found many strange things. One doctor in Bradford discovered that half the children in the schools there had not changed their clothes for six months! They had been specially wrapped up against the cold winter weather.

Children's health — then and now

This photograph shows children in London about 100 years ago. They look very poor and neglected.

Look carefully at the picture and describe the children.

Look at their clothes. Do they look happy? Do they look warm? Do they look clean and healthy? Do they look well-fed?

Make a survey of the kinds of food eaten by the children in your class for one day (include breakfast, lunch, tea and supper). What drinks do you have?

What do you eat between meals — at playtimes, going home from school, watching television?

Compare this classroom with your own. The photograph was taken about 100 years ago. Do you think

that the room looks bright, attractive, light and clean?
that the children have enough room to work in?
that there are any open spaces in the classroom?

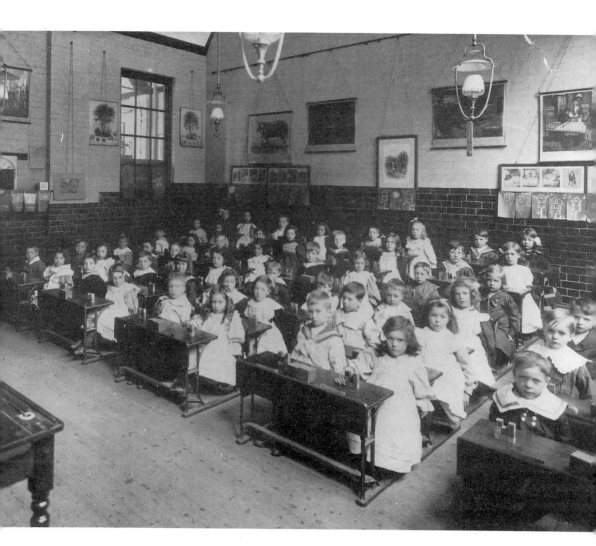

Do the desks look comfortable? They are like the desks in this old advertisement.

To Managers of National and other Schools, Mechanics Institutions, Working Men's Clubs, &c.

By Her Majesty's Royal Letters Patent.

BANKS'S PATENT SCHOOL DESK,

Convertible instantly into a Comfortable Seat or Table.

SOLE AGENT FOR HUDDERSFIELD AND NEIGHBOURHOOD,

Geo. TINDALL,

Bookseller, Printer, & Stationer,

No. 12, NEW STREET,

WHERE SPECIMENS OF THE DESKS MAY BE SEEN.

These Desks possess many important advantages over any other Furniture in use, among which may be mentioned free passage both before and behind the Seats, when arranged either as Desks or Tables.

Today's schoolchildren are healthier than they were 100 years ago. This chapter gives you some clues about the reasons.

Plague

On June 24th 1348 two ships sailed quietly into the tiny harbour of Melbourne Regis in Dorset on the south coast of England. (Today it the seaside town of Weymouth.) Although they did not know it, some of the sailors on board the ships were already suffering from the Black Death or plague.

Soon the disease was spreading quickly through Britain. The *epidemic* (large outbreak) of the plague lasted about three years. Historians think that it killed about 2½ million people in Britain. When you think that the total population was only about 4¾ million people this means that about half the population was wiped out! Millions more died in Europe in countries like France and Germany. We will never know exactly how many people caught the awful disease and died.

Do you think such a disaster could happen today? How would it affect you even though you survived? What would happen to our towns and cities?

People both rich and poor lived in great terror of the plague. They could not understand it. They did not know where it had come from or how to prevent it or cure it. They did not know its cause.

Artists painted frightening pictures of grinning skeletons and devils. These poor villagers are running away from Death on his horse. He is carrying a great weapon to chop them down. It is all happening at a cross-roads. These were supposed to be magical, mysterious places. The big birds are ravens.

People learned to live with the fear of death all round them. The plague became an *endemic* disease in Britain. This means that it was always present somewhere and always likely to flare up and cause another outbreak or epidemic.

The evidence

There is *archaeological* evidence being uncovered today about the plague. This is a recent newspaper report about a site in London where they have found a grave for victims of the Black Death in 1349.

Uncovering Black Death's grave of a thousand corpses

An excavation said to be the largest and most important in England is yielding a fascinating insight into the lives and deaths of Londoners during the Black Death, which killed nearly half the capital's population, up to 50,000 people, in the year 1349.

The dig, costing £1 million, is on the site of the old Royal Mint near the Tower of London, where more than 1,000 corpses are thought to be buried.

Archaelogists have uncovered orderly rows of graves which merge with a hastily filled gravel pit, made as the disease, bubonic plague, swept London.

Only one small metal belt clasp and traces of shrouds have been found in the graves.

Mr Peter Mills, field officer of the Museum of London, said yesterday: "We assume grave-diggers would help themselves to anything of value such as rings and brooches as a perk of the job and perks must have been few at the time".

The skeletons are being analysed to determine sex, height and age, and for any traces of arthritis, tuberculosis or other diseases.

They will then be re-buried in east London.

Records began to be kept to show the number of births and deaths. Here is some information from the first records ever kept to show the births and deaths in the city of London. They are for the years 1578 to 1582. The number of christenings or baptisms is very similar to the number of births because babies were usually baptised as soon as possible, before they could die of disease.

Abstracts of Burials and Baptisms in London, 1578–1583.

1578									
Month	Dead	Of plague	Of other diseases	Christened	Month	Dead	Of plague	Of other diseases	Christened
Jan.	392	91	301	301	July	518	212	306	260
Feb.	374	87	287	271	Aug.	721	398	323	269
Mar.	283	36	247	228	Sept.	1192	723	469	288
Apr.	378	112	266	259	Oct.	1400	873	527	269
May	594	171	423	238	Nov.	1093	534	559	326
June	341	125	216	194	Dec.	544	206	338	259
					TOTAL	7830	3568	4262	3162

1579									
Month	Dead	Of plague	Of other diseases	Christened	Month	Dead	Of plague	Of other diseases	Christened
Jan.	384	84	300	352	July	336	64	272	298
Feb.	304	64	240	247	Aug.	267	52	215	247
Mar.	253	45	208	276	Sept.	261	58	203	263
Apr.	369	88	281	286	Oct.	285	47	238	334
May	285	51	234	194	Nov.	188	18	170	288
June	254	41	213	207	Dec.	240	17	223	378
					TOTAL	3426	629	2797	3370

1580

Month	Dead	Of plague	Of other diseases	Christened	Month	Dead	Of plague	Of other diseases	Christened
Jan.	185	12	173	273	July	452	16	436	256
Feb.	198	13	185	321	Aug.	241	13	228	258
Mar.	248	8	240	353	Sept.	252	6	246	359
Apr.	184	4	180	304	Oct.	164	8	156	255
May	196	3	193	288	Nov.	221	17	204	287
June	225	9	216	289	Dec.	307	19	288	325
					TOTAL	2873	128	2745	3568

1581

Month	Dead	Of plague	Of other diseases	Christened	Month	Dead	Of plague	Of other diseases	Christened
Jan.	191	11	180	252	July	330	61	269	285
Feb.	191	7	184	258	Aug.	677	217	460	332
Mar.	253	8	245	379	Sept.	787	307	480	256
Apr.	163	6	157	193	Oct.	651	258	393	322
May	197	15	182	223	Nov.	[Figures not known]			
June	283	26	257	303	Dec.				
					TOTAL	3723	916	2807	2803
						[10 months]			

1582

Month	Dead	Of plague	Of other diseases	Christened	Month	Dead	Of plague	Of other diseases	Christened
Jan.	275	50	225	296	July	327	106	221	246
Feb.	302	43	259	305	Aug.	712	353	359	346
Mar.	366	62	304	383	Sept.	1019	624	395	292
Apr.	338	74	264	262	Oct.	1185	732	453	278
May	343	71	272	302	Nov.	1230	621	609	350
June	244	46	198	226	Dec.	[Figures not known]			
					TOTAL	6341	2782	3559	3286
						[11 months]			

Use the figures on the previous pages to draw a graph to show the following:

the number of deaths caused by plague each year
the total number of deaths each year
the number of christenings, (similar to the number of births), each year.

Which months were the worst for plague deaths?

Was there any year when there were no plague deaths?

What was happening to the population of London during these years? What do you think was the cause of this?

After 1583 the plague disappeared from London for about nine years. During that time the population of the city went up from 120 000 to 150 000.

The Great Plague

The plague struck again particularly badly in 1665 when it became known as the Great Plague.

Several people kept diaries during that terrible time. Two of them were doctors called Boghurst and Vincent. Why do you think their evidence is particularly interesting and important?

But the man who kept the best and most famous diary was called Samuel Pepys. As the plague grew worse in the summer of 1665 he wrote:

Great fears of the Sicknesse here in the City. God preserve us all.

Memory of the past is also important evidence. Everyone can remember things which have happened in the past. What is your oldest memory? Ask grown-ups at home what their oldest memories are.

One man wrote a book about the great London plague by using other people's memories. He listened carefully to the stories told by people who remembered it. Then he wrote all their memories down in a book which he called *A Journal of the Plague Year*. This was published many years after the Great Plague, in 1722.

The author's name was Daniel Defoe. In one part of the book he pretends to visit a place where the plague bodies are being buried.

It was about the 10th of September that my curiosity led or rather drove me to go and see this pit again ... and heard the bellman and then appeared a dead-cart ... but the buriers had covered the bodies so immediately with throwing in earth that though there was light enough ... there were lanterns and candles in them placed all night round the sides of the pit upon heaps of earth ...

This description was based on the memories of other people. Which is best — memory or the evidence written in diaries at the time the plague was happening?

The bodies were simply dumped into carts and then hurriedly thrown into the pits. Can you think why? The bodies were not even put into coffins. Why do you think this was?

An Order made by the City Council had forbidden any burials during the day. Can you think of a reason?

This Order had changed by the autumn. Dr Vincent wrote in his diary:

The nights are too short to bury the dead and we can hardly go forth but we should meet many coffins — one woman carrying a little coffin under her arm.

What is so sad about the poor woman mentioned by Dr Vincent?

The City Council kept written records which help us to understand the full horror of the plague. Each week a *Bill of Mortality* was published by the Council showing the number of deaths in the city, and the causes. The figures were collected by parish clerks.

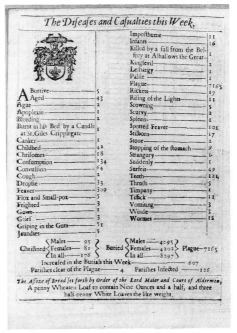

How many people died of plague on this Bill?

How many births were there in the week? (Remember that christenings are probably the same as births.) How many deaths? Were there more births than deaths?

Some of the causes of death seem strange to us. What do you think 'surfeit', 'griping in the guts', 'teeth' and 'frighted' meant?

Do you think that some of the deaths described as of 'feaver' may really have been of plague?

A historian who was writing in the 1890s, Dr Creighton, compiled a list giving the number of people who died of the plague in London during 1665. He made it from records like the Bill of Mortality on page 17. Do you think his list is accurate? (Clue: look back at the last paragraph.)

Bill of Mortality of the Plague-year 1665 in London.

Month	Christened	Buried	Plague	Month	Christened	Buried	Plague
Jan.	1150	2041	0	July	791	6820	4127
Feb.	910	1644	1	Aug.	899	25,427	19,046
Mar.	931	1590	0	Sept.	657	30,699	26,230
Apr.	1003	1468	2	Oct.	638	17,201	14,373
May	1135	1873	43	Nov.	428	4595	3449
June	843	2262	590	Dec.	403	1395	734
				TOTAL	9788	97,015	68,595

Make a large block graph showing the number of births and the number of plague deaths in each month.

In which month did the plague begin?

In which month did the disease begin to gather force?

When do you think the people of London began to get really worried?

When were the first signs that the plague was beginning to die down?

Look at the prints at the top of the following page.

Which one shows the burial of a rich or important person and which one shows how less important people were buried?

How do you think, even less fortunate people were buried? (Clue: look at page 17.)

In the left-hand picture a man has collapsed and died on the burial ground. Is anyone taking any notice of him? What does this tell you?

London, normally a city of bustle and noise, became a place of death and horror. Pepys describes a city which is more like a ghost town:

> What a sad time it is to all; no boats upon the river and grass grows all up and down Whitehall Court and nobody but poor wretches in the streets.

What does the evidence of the grass growing in the street tell you?

Who do you think the 'poor wretches' were?

Many Londoners were so frightened they left the city as soon as they could. They fled to the safety of the villages in the countryside round London.

This picture shows a queue of people trying to get into a local village. In the distance you can see London. Why do you think there are guards at the village entrance? The man at the front of the queue is showing the guard a piece of paper on which a doctor has probably written to say he was free of plague. If you were a guard would you believe him?

19

Make your own *broadsheet* or newspaper about the plague. You will need to find reference books about the 1665 plague in your library, as well as using this book. Report on the numbers of deaths. Here are two examples from school children to give you ideas.

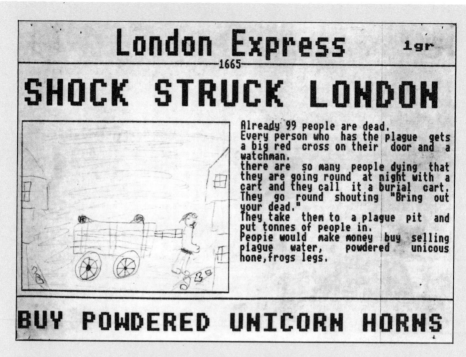

London Express
1665

SHOCK STRUCK LONDON

Already 99 people are dead.
Every person who has the plague gets a big red cross on their door and a watchman.
there are so many people dying that they are going round at night with a cart and they call it a burial cart. They go round shouting "Bring out your dead."
They take them to a plague pit and put tonnes of people in.
Peopie would make money buy selling plague water, powdered unicous hone, frogs legs.

BUY POWDERED UNICORN HORNS

LONDON TIMES
SEPTEMBER 1665

GREAT PLAGUE KILLS MOST OF LONDON

A disease is killing most of LONDON'S population 1000 a day are dying so far 7000 have died. We are expecting many more to die.

Yesterday the king found a body in his his house of easement .

s

Buy frogs' legs for a cure

Symptoms

Dr Boghurst and Daniel Defoe both tell us about the *symptoms* of the plague. Dr Boghurst wrote:

> Some died in twelve or twenty days but most in five or six. The botches or buboes [swellings or lumps] were the most distinctive signs of the plague having given to it the old name of 'the botch'. Besides these there were the 'tokens' [red spots which spread across the skin]. Tokens come out after a violent sweat.

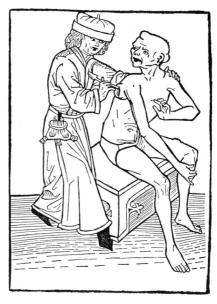

In this print of 1482 a 'bubo' is being pierced to cure it

Defoe wrote:

> Some were overwhelmed and it came with violent fever, vomiting, headaches, pains in the back ... others with swellings and tumours ... which put them in agonies and torment while others were silently infected until they fell swooning and fainting.

If you were a plague doctor what would you look for as a sign of the plague?

Other evidence

Evidence of the plague has survived in a nursery rhyme and game which you have probably played. Here is the song children sing as they play — not knowing that they are singing about the plague:

> Ring-a-ring of roses
> A pocket full of posies,
> Atishoo! Atishoo!
> We all fall down.

Can you explain the rhyme? The second line mentions posies. This means small bunches of flowers. People often carried them because they believed the sweet smell of the flowers would keep away the plague. (Clue: the roses mentioned are not flowers. Could they refer to the 'tokens'?)

21

The fight against the plague

In the last chapter you got some idea of what a plague epidemic was like. On everyone's lips were questions:

Where does the plague come from?
How is it caused?
How does it spread?
How can it be avoided?

There were plenty of ideas about what caused the plague and how to avoid it. Here are just a few of them and the dates when they were written.

1500   Avoid anything rotten or stinking.
Avoid the southerly wind.
Let your house be kept clean.
Let your house be sprinkled with vinegar and roses.
Wash your hands often.

1543   All streets and lanes should be kept clean.

1543   All persons having dogs should have them killed and buried outside the city.

1593   Fires should be made in the streets every morning.

1603   The plague comes out of holes in the soil. When rats and moles and other creatures leave their holes it is a sign of corruption [rottenness].

For thousands of years people have searched for clues to find the causes and cures of illnesses like the plague. They have followed clues but sometimes they have not understood them properly. Sometimes they have followed the wrong clues. Sometimes they haven't even recognised the clues when they have seen them. The search for answers sometimes takes hundreds of years. The plague is a good example.

One of the first books to be printed in England, in about 1480, was about the plague. By then it was endemic in this country and in Europe.

The book gave the advice of a Danish bishop:

> In pestilence [plague] time nobody should stand in great press of people [crowds], because some man of them may be infect. Therefore wise physicians, in visiting sick folk, stand far from the patient, holding their face toward the door or window ... Also it is good to a patient every day for to change his chamber, and often times to have the windows open against the North and East, and to spar [close] the windows against the South. For the south wind hath two causes of putrefaction [rottenness]. The first is, it maketh a man, being whole or sick, feeble in their bodies. The second cause is ... the south wind grieveth the hearing and hurteth the heart, because it openeth the pores of man and entereth into the heart.

What is the bishop's idea of how the plague gets into the body?

Why should the south wind make people feel feeble? (Clue: winds from the south are usually warm.)

What did he think was good about the east and north winds? Why were they different from the south wind?

In 1894, (more than 400 years later, but less than 100 years ago), Dr Creighton wrote this in a book he was writing about diseases:

> The ... plague is a poison coming from the soil. Plague lives in and comes from the soil.

This is like one of the ideas on page 22. Which one?

What does this tell you about the progress people made in the search for the answers to the plague in 300 years?

Dr Creighton looked carefully at the evidence of the plague which had arrived in the tiny village of Eyam in Derbyshire in the summer of 1665. He noticed that the records showed that the disease seemed to die out in winter and then break out again the following summer. He wondered why. This was his answer:

> The virus [germ] must have passed into the pores of the ground after the first 60 or more burials in the churchyard down to the lull of the epidemic in winter; with the rise of the ground-water in spring, it would be ... inactive; but in June, when the water was again sinking in the soil and the great heat was raising emanations [discharges] from the dry ground, it broke forth [and] poisoned the whole air of the valley.

23

The real cause

Soon after Dr Creighton wrote his book scientists discovered the real answer to the cause of the plague.

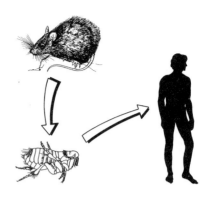

The disease first begins in certain types of rat. It is spread by fleas which bite the infected rat and then bite other rats or human beings so causing infection.

The rats lived in the filth and dirt of the streets and alleys of towns and cities like London. This old drawing gives you an idea of what conditions were like. Describe what is happening in the picture.

Rubbish and sewage were thrown into the streets and piled up in the alleys. People drank water polluted by the filth. Thousands of rats lived and bred in these dirty conditions.

Rats were not the only cause of plague. They caused the kind we call *bubonic*, after the buboes or lumps which appeared on the body. There was probably another form of plague which we now call *pneumonic* plague. This was even worse than bubonic because the germs which caused it could pass directly from one person to another and attack their lungs.

Friar Clyn, writing in Ireland more than 500 years ago, seems to have noticed that there were two kinds of plague:

> Many died from boils and botches which grew on the legs and under the arms ... others died by vomiting blood.

Can you find the two different forms in what Defoe said on page 21?

Like Dr Creighton, the Londoners of 1665 blamed poisoned air, dampness and mist which they saw rising from stale water and marshes and ponds. They believed bad smells also had something to do with the plague. They were following the right clues but not going far enough. They had never heard of germs. Germs which can be deadly but which cannot be seen. Germs which grow and breed in dirt.

Precautions against the plague

To stop the plague people lit great fires in the London streets. Can you think why?

People were ordered to kill their cats, dogs, rabbits, pigeons and pigs. Do you think this would have helped to clean up the streets? What would be the effect of killing all the dogs and cats? (Look back at the diagram on page 24 for a clue.)

Watchmen were sent to guard houses where the plague had broken out. People living there were locked into their homes and not allowed out for forty days. Healthy people were shut in with those who were dying of the disease. Do you think this was a good idea? What do you think many people did to avoid being locked away in a plague house?

25

This picture, drawn in 1665, shows some of the precautions taken.

How many guards are outside houses locked up because of the disease?

Count the crosses on the doors. A cross was a sign of plague in the house.

Notice the two women carrying long sticks. They were called *searchers*. They had to visit houses where people had the plague so that they could keep a count of the deaths from the disease. Would you have told the searchers about anyone with plague in your house? What might happen if you were honest?

Try making a model of a plague house with a red cross on the door and a watchman in the street. Here is one which some children made.

Here are some entries from Samuel Pepys's diary. Make a list of the fears Pepys had of the plague and any precautions he or the City Council took to avoid the disease.

> *June 7th, 1665.*   This day, much against my Will, I did in Drury lane see two or three houses marked with a red cross upon the doors, and 'Lord have mercy upon us' writ there — which was a sad sight to me ... It put me into an ill conception of myself [made me feel worried about myself] and my smell, so that I was forced to by some roll-tobacco to smell and to chaw [chew] — which took away the apprehension [fear].

What did he mean by his 'smell'?

Samuel Pepys

> *September 3rd.* Up, and put on my coloured silk suit, very fine, and my new periwigg, bought a good while since, but darst not wear it because the plague was in Westminster when I bought it. And it is a wonder what will be the fashion after the plague is done as to periwigs, for nobody will dare to buy any haire for fear of the infection — that it had been cut off of the heads of people dead of the plague.

> *September 14th.*   I did endeavour [try] to talk with as few as I could, there being now no ... shutting up of houses infected, that to be sure we do converse and meet with people that have the plague upon them.

> *November 4th.*   My head a little akeing, partly for want of natural rest ... and partly from the news I hear, that one of the little boys at my lodging is not well, and they suspect ... that it may be the plague ... I was resolved myself to abstain [stop] coming thither for a while.

> *January 30, 1666.*   This is the first time I have been in this church since I left London for the plague; and it frighted me indeed to go through the church, more than I thought it would have done, to see so many graves lie so high upon the churchyard, where people have been buried of the plague. I was much troubled at it, and do not think to go through it again a good while.

Even little children were sometimes forced to smoke pipes of tobacco. Why should people like Pepys think chewing and smoking tobacco would prevent the plague?

Doctors who tended the plague victims took great precautions and dressed themselves in strange costumes. They must have frightened more patients than they cured!

This picture shows a plague doctor.

Why is he wearing long clothes, boots and gloves? His bird-mask is filled with sweet-smelling herbs and dried flowers. Why?

When people are frightened or very ill they will try anything which might protect or cure them.

Below is a charm some people wore round their necks to keep away the plague. Would you expect it to work?

```
A B R A C A D A B R A
A B R A C A D A B R
A B R A C A D A B
A B R A C A D A
A B R A C A D
A B R A C A
A B R A C
A B R A
A B R
A B
A
```

Make up an advertisement for your own fake or 'quack' medicine. Try and persuade people to buy it.

Here are two examples which some children made up.

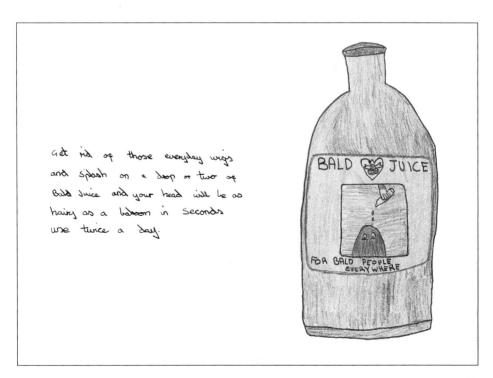

This Brilliant medicene Makes spots disappear in seconds. IF you take this medicane 4 times a day you'll never ever get any Spots. It comes with a free spoon Price: 2 Shillings

Spotty!
Spotty makes Spots disappear
Take this 4 times a day

Get rid of those everyday wigs and splash on a drop or two of Bald Juice and your head will be as hairy as a baboon in seconds use twice a day.

BALD JUICE
FOR BALD PEOPLE EVERYWHERE

Dirty water and disease

The following newspaper report appeared in January 1987. After days of great cold and frost the weather suddenly turned milder. The warm air brought a thaw and that caused thousands of burst water pipes in houses, offices and factories. Deep in the ground, mains pipes carrying water from the reservoirs also cracked and burst. That brought water shortages to many towns.

Read the account, and make a list of the dangers the burst pipes brought.

What did the Water Authorities do to help people?

Water tankers called in to beat shortages

THOUSANDS of families in London and the West Country face serious water shortages as millions of gallons run to waste through burst pipes.

A fleet of water tankers yesterday took emergency supplies to London hospitals, while tankers also supplied people in West Cornwall.

In the West Country families were urged to adopt 'drought-like' restrictions. Some homes in Devon and Cornwall were without water altogether, while others were on greatly reduced pressure.

But the Thames authority denied that low water pressure could cause explosions in gas water heaters, geysers and back-fired boilers. As a precaution, however, heaters should be turned off when not in use.

'Although we have been suffering burst water mains at the rate of 100 a day, most of the water is being lost through unlagged burst pipes in the home. Mains pipes have been repaired within 24 hours,' said Mr Christopher Bailey, the authority's spokesman.

Imagine what would happen if the water supply to your school was cut off for a month. Where would you go for water? How would you manage? What difficulties would there be?

Make a group plan showing your school and the places you could go to get water. Decide first what you would need water for. How would you organise trips to get it?

Today when we want water we simply turn a tap. With a partner make a list of the things you use water for at home. How many taps do you each have at home?

In the past things were very different. A hundred years ago many people had to get their water from springs, ponds and rivers. In the towns poor people had to queue at street pumps. Can you imagine having to walk about a quarter of a mile carrying water in a bucket? Would it encourage you to keep very clean?

People queuing at a street pump in London in the 1860s

In Burton-on-Trent a hundred years ago poor families used only nine buckets of water each week. That was for a family of about five people and included washing clothes, cooking, cleaning, drinking and washing. How much water do you think you use each day? (For example, each time you flush the toilet you use one bucketful of water.)

Water is very important to us. For drinking and cooking it must be clean. Today our water is supplied from huge reservoirs often many miles away from our taps. It is carefully cleaned, filtered and tested before we use it.

31

In the past people had little idea where their water came from before they pumped it out from a well or sank their bucket in a river or pond. Often the water they drank and cooked with was poisoned or *polluted* with sewage or rubbish. Butchers, grocers, tanners — in fact everybody — threw their rubbish into the streets and gutters. If there was a river or stream nearby the rubbish was thrown into the water together with buckets of sewage and household rubbish. Generally the same river or stream was used for drinking water.

Jacob's Island, Bermondsey in 1800. The wooden shacks were either privies or pigsties which emptied into the stream. The stream was also used for drinking water!

Cholera

A new and terrible disease came to Britain from India which was first recognised in 1831. The disease was *cholera*.

People who caught cholera suffered violent stomach pains. They were sick and they shivered with cold until their skins turned blue. Sometimes the disease killed people within two hours.

This chart shows the effect of the cholera epidemic of 1832 in Glasgow. Make a block graph to show the growth of the disease and compare the deaths from cholera with the total of deaths from all causes.

Glasgow Mortality in 1832.

	All deaths	Cholera deaths		All deaths	Cholera deaths
Jan.	824	—	July	990	441
Feb.	874	87	Aug.	1755	1222
March	955	264	Sept.	749	243
April	816	229	Oct.	755	334
May	677	125	Nov.	529	25
June	783	196	Dec.	571	—
			TOTAL	10 278	3166

The epidemic died away and people hoped it would never return.

Doctors, like everyone else, did not understand the disease. They argued about its causes. Bad smells were often blamed. People called this *miasma*.

One man was following the clues just a little bit further than everyone else. His name was Edwin Chadwick. He wanted to see the filthy towns and cities cleared completely of their rubbish and sewage. He wanted to see everyone with a clean water-supply and all homes connected with sewers.

But Chadwick made a mistake. He believed that miasma — bad smells — caused disease. New sewers were built in parts of London and Chadwick fought to have them regularly flushed with water to get rid of the smells. The sewers were flushed. And the sewage was pumped straight into the River Thames — which many people used for drinking water.

Sewers being built in 1862

33

In 1832 microscopes were not powerful enough to show germs, although scientists did know that microscopic (extremely tiny) animals did exist. These had been discovered more than a hundred years before by a Dutchman called Leeuwenhook, who had called them 'wee animals'. Some doctors were even beginning to think the invisible animals could fly through the air and carry disease with them.

The search went on. Clues were followed. Clues were ignored. But the man who followed them in the right direction was John Snow, a London surgeon. He pieced all the clues together.

From observing people who were already suffering from cholera, he noticed that cholera always began with badly upset stomachs.

The clues John Snow was studying led him to a group of patients who had all drunk from the same water supply. The water was polluted by sewage.

Snow thought he had found the answer. He published a book about it in 1849, but scientists and doctors did not believe him.

Five years passed and the cholera epidemic struck again, but this time Snow was ready. He studied carefully what was happening in one area of London where the houses were supplied with piped water by two different water companies. One was the Vauxhall Water Company, the other the Lambeth Water Company.

The first company pumped its water from the River Thames at a place where the river was thick with human sewage. The second took its water from the Thames as well, but from a part of the river which was clear of pollution. None of the people who drank the water knew where it was coming from. These *statistics* show what John Snow discovered.

Houses supplied by Vauxhall Water Company — 266 516
Cholera deaths in 14 weeks — 4093

Houses supplied by Lambeth Water Company — 173 748
Cholera deaths in 14 weeks — 451

Which water company would you prefer to get your water from?

John Snow wrote:

Part of the water has passed through the kidneys and bowels of 2 million and a quarter of the inhabitants of London
Medical Times, 30th September, 1854

Some people in Broad Street in London began to fall ill with cholera. Snow investigated. He found they all got their water from a local street pump. Then he found out that just before the illness began a child had died in one of the houses in Broad Street. The child had died of diarrhoea. The child's nappies had been washed in water which had been poured away down a sink. The drain it went down lead to a pool of sewage which soaked slowly into the ground and ended up being pumped up again as drinking water at the Broad Street pump. The people in Broad Street were drinking sewage!

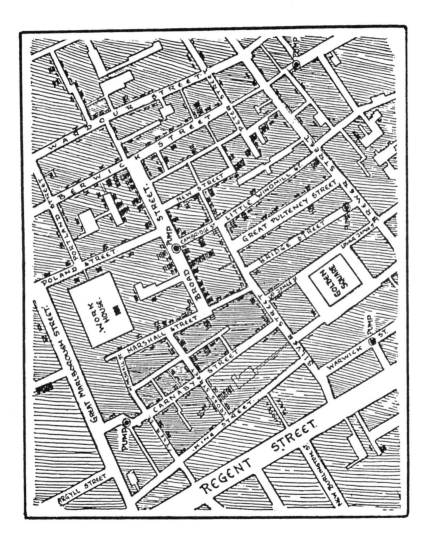

Part of Snow's map showing the position of the Broad Street pump. The slanting lines within the blocks of houses stand for deaths from cholera in each house.

People sometimes call the River Thames 'Old Father Thames', as if the river was an old man. This is how one artist imagined the old man a hundred years ago. Can you explain why? What can you see in the picture?

Father Thames with his 'children'

Housing and health

About 200 years ago thousands of families began to move from villages to live in new towns and seek work in factories and mines. The homes they left behind in the country were often tumble-down and dirty. Some people even shared their cottages with pigs and cattle. The homes they found in the towns were just as bad — in many cases worse.

The population of the towns grew rapidly, which led to overcrowding and the spread of more disease. This picture shows conditions in which people lived in London in 1872.

What things would affect the health of the people?

This photograph was taken in Glasgow about a hundred years ago. Sewage and slops were thrown into the gutter in the middle of the court. Can you find the water supply for the houses?

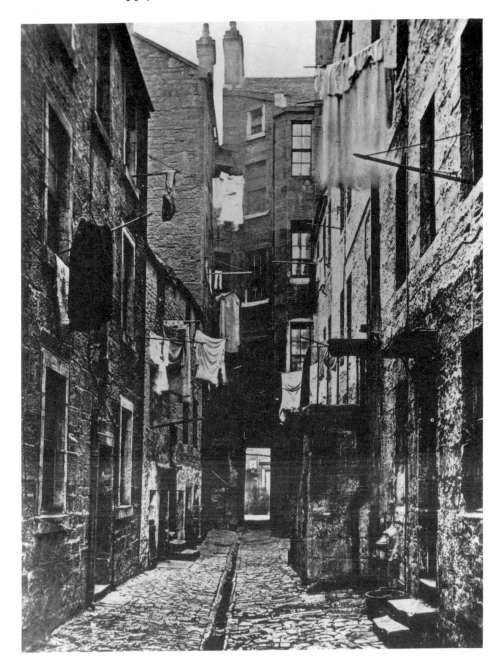

Compare this with the streets near your home or school. Do you know of any streets like this?

Read this description of a street in Stockport about 150 years ago.

> Two rows of houses with a street seven yards wide between them; each row consists of what are styled back and front houses—that is two houses placed back to back. There are no yards ... the privies [lavatories] are in the centre of each row, about a yard wide; over them there is part of a sleeping-room; there is no ventilation in the bedrooms; each house contains two rooms ... a house place [living room] and sleeping room above; each room is about three yards wide and four long. In one of these houses there are nine persons belonging to one family, and the mother on the eve of her confinement [about to have a baby]. There are 44 houses in the two rows, and 22 cellars, all of the same size. The cellars are let off as separate dwellings; these are dark, damp, and very low, not more than six feet between the ceiling and the floor. The street between the two rows is seven yards wide, in the centre of which is the common gutter, or more properly sink, into which all sorts of refuse is thrown ...

In your classroom or hall measure out the area of one of the rooms. What would it be like with nine people in it? Try it out with nine of you standing in the area you have measured. The cellars would be similar—but with only one room for eating and sleeping in.

Cramped living conditions

The people who lived here were fairly lucky — at least they had some lavatories. Many streets built at about that time in the new towns of factories, steelworks and workshops did not have any at all. People kept their sewage in buckets and bowls in their homes. Then, when the buckets were full, the sewage was emptied out into the streets or thrown on to big piles of rubbish or into ponds and pits called cesspits. Huge piles of filth collected in the streets and the wetness seeped into the cellars where people lived. In one part of the town of Gateshead there were just three privies for 2000 people.

Hundreds of people lived in the two rows in Stockport. How many toilets would there be do you think? (Two yards wide altogether.) These would be holes with buckets underneath. Make a scale drawing showing the houses, rows, the width of the street and the gutter (perhaps half a yard wide).

There is no mention of one very important thing in the street in Stockport. Can you think what it was? (Clue: look back to the last chapter.)

Scavengers

Men who had to empty the privies, dig away the dung hills and empty the cesspools were called scavengers. These are the details from Huddersfield:

DAY SCAVENGING

MONTH.	CENTRAL DISTRICT.								BOROUGH.	
	Loads of Street Sweepings Removed.	Loads of Slop from Streets.	Loads of Refuse from Markets and Shops.	Loads of Saleable Manure Removed.	Loads of Water for Street Watering Purposes.	Loads of Ashes spread during frosty weather.	Loads of Snow removed from Streets.	Total No. of Loads Removed.	Loads of Ashes from Dry Ashpits.	Total No. of Loads of Refuse from Ashpits
1879.										
January	–	52	59	94	–	33	274	512	253	889
February	13	284	40	51	–	7	215	610	179	754
March	46	116	49	59	–	–	309	579	224	663
April	86	125	50	27	–	–	–	288	248	877½
May	161	46	56	18	446	–	–	727	239½	861
June	152	50	59	32	400	–	–	693	147	785
July	151	76	79	8	319	–	–	633	156½	548
August	114	96	78	7½	574	–	–	869½	154	561
September	162	62	72	46	191	–	–	533	134¼	693
October	91	136	74	23	–	–	–	324	205	781
November	98½	112	54	15½	–	–	–	280	167	755
December	10	14	55	14	–	–	53	146	396	965
Total	1084½	1169	725	395	1930	40	851	6194½	2503¼	9132½

MONTH.	CENTRAL DISTRICT.				OUTER DISTRICTS.			
	Night Soil.	Refuse.	Water.	Total.	Night Soil.	Refuse.	Water.	Total.
1879.								
January	90	581	2	673	215	532	5	752
February	76	374	4	454	359	441	3	803
March	94	420	4	518	335	414	2	751
April	124	460	7	591	376	468	2	846
May	93	390	1	484	285	482	5	772
June	23	448	2	473	202	517	6	725
July	3	429	8	440	76	641	16	733
August	2	308	6	316	108	585	6	699
September	22	371	1	394	158	566	6	730
October	40	361	2	403	109	500	6	615
November	18	387	–	405	96	594	16	706
December	23	414	2	439	123	509	2	634
Total for 1879	608	4943	39	5590	2442	6249	75	8766

What do you think happened to the manure collected by the scavengers?

What else did they have to remove?

Scavengers at work emptying privies

Often towns and cities sold human sewage to farmers for manuring their fields. Night scavengers took away human sewage (called night soil) which they tipped into carts. Why do you think it was taken away at night?

Many streets were never cleaned at all because they were too narrow for the scavengers' carts.

Tuberculosis

People living in such unhealthy places must have been very sickly and pale. Diseases spread easily in such conditions and the one that killed the most people was tuberculosis, sometimes called 'the white plague'.

Tuberculosis attacks every part of the body, but particularly the lungs. Today we know that the white plague was spread from one person to another through coughs and sneezes. In the past people did not understand this and so the disease spread, especially where people were living in stuffy, dirty and overcrowded homes.

Tuberculosis was doubly dangerous because it could be caught by animals and particularly cows. When cows caught the disease their milk became infected. Can you guess what happened then?

Here is part of the Halifax medical officer of health's report for 1875. (*Pulmonary* means affecting the lungs and *zymotic* means infectious.) Look up the places on the map opposite.

> Ovenden Ward has the highest pulmonary death rate, but it has the lowest zymotic rate; Northowram is also high, with a zymotic rate below the average: West is the same. These facts, in my opinion, admit of only one explanation, viz., that the highest and most exposed parts of the borough suffer most from pulmonary affections. And, indeed, this cannot be surprising, for the biting winds and cold, whether from the east or west, must be more piercing at Queen's-road, Pellon, and Claremount, than they are in East or South Wards. It is better then for those who have bronchial troubles to avoid exposed situations, and if they could nestle under 'Old Father Beacon', [a large hill], the probabilities are they would have a longer lease of life than in some more salubrious [healthy], yet somewhat bleak situations. For the same reason North Ward, with a dense population of nearly all factory workers, and surrounded by many sanitary defects and unhealthy conditions, has a pulmonary death rate four per cent below the average.

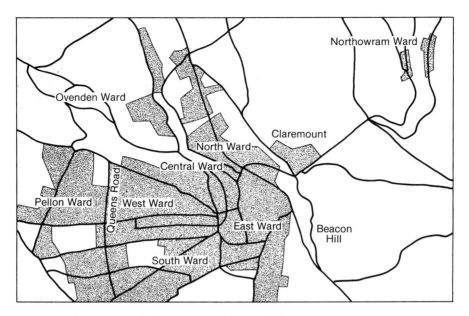

A map showing the different wards in Halifax

A sanitary inspector went round over 3000 houses and found the following:

Sink pipes communicating directly with sewers	1 011
Houses with deficient privy accommodation	668
Houses overcrowded	78
Houses in a filthy condition	47
Houses with only one bed-room	1 997

Can it be a matter of surprise that fever is never absent from the town when nearly one-third of the houses inspected have sink pipes untrapped; that is, a direct communication between the sewers and the dwelling?

The result is, that 'drain fever' or as it is commonly called, 'typhoid,' is the prevailing zymotic disease of the town, and numbers more than all the rest.

In which parts of the town did people suffer most from zymotic disease — the high or low parts?

The medical officer thought people should live where it was warmer, under 'Old Father Beacon'.

The people of the North Ward did not suffer so much from pulmonary diseases. What kind do you think they suffered from? Look at the medical officer's list and what he says about it. Were most people living in healthy or unhealthy conditions? What improvements were needed?

43

Babies and children

Grandmother, Grandmother,
Tell me the truth.
How many years am I
Going to live?
One. Two. Three. Four ...

Those are the words from an old skipping chant. Do you think they are sad? Imagine children in the playground chanting and counting. Every number meant another year of life.

In 1884 the medical officer in Halifax wrote this in his report. It had been a bad year for babies. What reasons does he give for the deaths? You will need a dictionary.

> With regard to the causes of infant mortality [deaths of babies] in Halifax it may be noted that 49 resulted from zymotic [infectious] causes (including 22 from diarrhoea, 12 from measles, six from whooping cough, and six from congenital syphilis), 18 from tubercular diseases, 43 from premature birth (an exceptionally high number), 106 from convulsions and brain affections, 93 from diseases of the respiratory organs, 23 from teething, and 78 from all other causes, mainly, atrophy, debility, and inanition.

Draw a block graph to show the causes of death.

Compare the medical officer's report with a similar report from Bradford for 1878:

Number of deaths of children under 1 year:

Atrophy/debilty	206	Pre-birth	128
Convulsions	190	Diarrhoea	118
Bronchitis	159	Whooping cough	58

You can see that many very young children were dying painful deaths.

A hundred years ago young mothers did not know how best to look after their babies. In 1883 the medical officer in Huddersfield wrote this:

> Many diseases are curable. Unfortunately many mothers are ignorant of the dangers of disease and the means of treatment. Measles is often treated by wrapping the child up when his body-heat is above normal

and then letting him expose himself to cold when his body-heat comes down again. The doctor is seldom called before this foolish treatment has caused bronchitis or pneumonia.

In Brussels I am told the registrar gives every mother a small handbill showing them how to look after babies. We should do the same. The handbill should tell mothers about food, clothing and proper ventilation of the baby's room. There should be directions of how to avoid disease. There could be other handbills about whooping cough and measles which could be delivered to every door in the areas of town where the diseases break out.

The medical officer was worried about ignorance and the way many mothers were treating their children suffering from measles.

What were the mothers doing wrong?

Do you think his idea for handbills was a good one?

Change takes a long time. Twenty years later, Huddersfield's medical officer was still worried by the number of infant deaths in the town. Read his advice. Do you agree with it?

What NOT to do.

NEVER give the baby soothing syrups, fever powders, or anything of that sort.

NEVER give the baby broad, or sops, or gravy, or any other food, except milk, till it is more than seven months old.

NEVER give the baby skimmed milk, or milk that is not perfectly fresh and good.

NEVER use a feeding bottle with a long tube. Nobody can keep the inside of the tube clean.

GOOD & BAD FEEDING BOTTLES

OUNCES

A GOOD KIND OF FEEDING BOTTLE BECAUSE IT CAN BE KEPT CLEAN | CALLED 'BABY KILLER' FORBIDDEN BY LAW IN FRANCE AS DANGEROUS & IMPOSSIBLE TO KEEP CLEAN CUT THE TUBE OPEN SMELL IT AND SEE!

NEVER use a 'comforter' or dummy teat. It is most injurious.

NEVER carry the baby 'sitting up' until it is five months old.

NEVER neglect to send for a Doctor if the baby is ill. Babies are soon overcome and easily die.

Do some research at home. Find out if adults agree with this advice, then collect your results and list the medical officer's ideas in four sections:

Agree
Disagree
Partly right
Nobody does this now

Perhaps you know someone who is going to have or has just had a baby. Ask how they are looked after. What advice do they have? Do they go to clinics or hospitals? Does a health visitor come to see them after the baby is born?

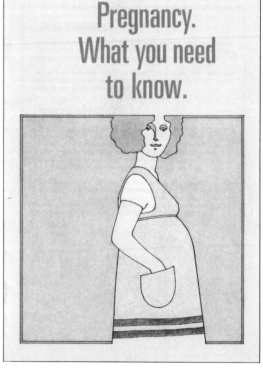

This cartoon shows another danger which threatened young children. Perhaps it will surprise you. Children often went into bars where they could drink and sometimes smoke as well.

How many children can you see in this cartoon?

How old do you think they are?

What do you think the woman is giving the baby she is carrying? Can you think why?

Notice the children's clothes.

Bad housing, poor food, dirt and ignorance all helped to kill children. The greatest killer of all was diarrhoea.

The medical officer in Bradford wrote this in his report in 1880:

> The influence of high temperature on the mortality from Diarrhoea is shewn in the following table, in which it will be seen that the deaths from Diarrhoea increased and diminished with the rise and fall of temperature:

Month	Temperature. °F			Rainfall in inches.	Deaths from Diarrhoea.
	Max.	Min.	Mean.		
July	70.7	49.7	57.7	7.74	14
August	79.3	49.5	60.4	1.3	57
September	81.3	45.0	59.0	3.89	122
October	68.3	26.7	55.8	4.7	50

> Of the 278 deaths from this disease, 253 were of children under five years of age, of whom 154 were infants under one year, and 73 between one and two years.

Using these figures, complete these graphs showing the temperature and diarrhoea deaths in Bradford in 1880. Which month has the lowest death rate? Which has the highest?

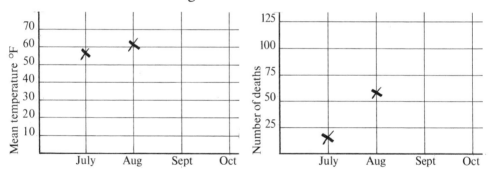

At what time of the year was diarrhoea at its worst? Can you think of any reasons?

Milk could be a great cause of disease. Can you remember from the last chapter which disease could get in cow's milk and affect people?

Poor people bought milk for their children because they thought it would do them good. Often the milk was full of germs. Sometimes the dairy or milkman took the cream out of the milk. Sometimes they poured in water and chalk to make it look rich and make it go further. The water added to the milk might be dirty and perhaps came from the farmyard pump.

Sometimes farmyard pumps were called 'the cow with the iron tail'. Can you explain this?

The medical officer in Halifax visited one dairy in 1904 and later wrote:

> Cows are kept in the most filthy conditions standing in manure in the cowsheds, the stalls are covered in manure and outside the yards are heaped with it. The milkers are filthy, their hands and clothes are dirty and their vessels very often are dirty.

People who sold milk were careless. Often it stood in containers into which dust and dirt dropped. Sometimes it was three or four days old before it was sold.

In Bradford a milk inspector discovered one shop where a bowl used for serving milk was also used as the baby's bath!

Read the medical officer's report for Bradford in 1878. You will need a dictionary.

> I have frequently remarked that rather than pass through the portions of street and passage necessary to reach the proper receptacle, women will conceal excreta in some obscure corner of the premises until nightfall. The effect of thus contaminating the already sufficiently close atmosphere of a back-to-back house, is of course exceedingly prejudicial [very harmful] to a child suffering from the effects of bad nursing and improper diet. More especially is this the case, when the obscure corner before mentioned, is beneath the shelf on which the milk is kept.
>
> It is a very common delusion in Bradford that a baby requires more substantial food than that which nature has provided. The result of this over-stuffing is diarrhoea and vomiting in the summer; convulsions, tabes mesenterica, atrophy, and of many deaths ascribed to 'teething' at other seasons of the year.
>
> In my opinion, the principal causes of the mortality among infants from autumnal diarrhoea (in Bradford at least) are improper feeding and general bad management, which have become traditional [usual] among a certain class, and the neglect to send for advice in the earlier stages of the disease.

What was happening to the sewage in houses without toilets?

Bad sanitary arrangements were causing many deaths. What was the other cause?

It often takes a long time to persuade people to change their ideas. Sometimes a *very* long time. This is what Dr Fordyce wrote in 1773:

> ... there must be near 20 000 children in London ... ill at this moment of the hectic fever [rickets] ... owing to the impure air which they breathe, the improper food on which they live ... they are fed even on meat before they have got their teeth ... or buttered rolls, or tough muffins floated in oiled butter ...

That was written before there were any medical officers. Yet Dr Fordyce was really giving the same advice as the Huddersfield medical officer (page 45) 130 years later.

Immunisation

In 1886 a terrible thing happened in Bradford. Read the story for yourself as it was reported by the medical officer. Hydrophobia means rabies. You will need a dictionary to look up some of the words.

HYDROPHOBIA.

One of the remarkable events of the year was the dispatch of a party of eight persons to Paris to undergo a course of Anti-rabie treatment at the hands of M. Pasteur. They had all been bitten by the same rabid dog, on January 24th, 1886, between the hours of 8.50 a.m. and 5.50 p.m., about which time the dog was killed. A man named Tom Ashworth who had been bitten by the dog on the same day, died of Hydrophobia on March 13th at the Workhouse, where he had been removed for treatment.

Mr Lodge, the police surgeon, and Mr Collins, veterinary surgeon to the Corporation, made a post-mortem examination of the dog next day, and found a quantity of straw, chips, and other miscellaneous matters [a variety of things] in its stomach, as is commonly the case with rabid dogs. Mr Lodge gave it as his opinion that the dog was rabid, and in this opinion Mr Collins concurred [agreed].

The condition of the other persons bitten by the dog was manifestly one of great peril [was dangerous]. The period of incubation of the virus in one case had already expired, leaving the victim dead. Which of the others would succumb next? Was there any means of preventing further deaths? These were the anxious questions for consideration.

As the result of consultation with Drs Proctor, Bell, and Foster, and after the matter had been considered by the Finance Committee, it was agreed that I should take the whole party at once to Paris, and that a subscription should be started to collect the necessary funds, the rates not being available for such a purpose. The appeal to the public of Bradford was as usual very generously answered. I accordingly started on March 15th, taking with me the following:

(1) Martha Hannah Wright, aged 10, Horton Green, bitten very severely on the calf of the left leg.
(2) Thomas Starkey, aged 7, 21 Granby Street, bitten in the right upper eyelid.
(3) James Hosty, aged 6, 51 Pollard Street, bitten on the left side of the mouth.
(4) Asa Moore, aged 6, 249 Horton Road, bitten in left fore arm.
(5) Swithenbank Turner, aged 8, 39 Shearbridge Terrace, bitten in the left leg.

(6) Thomas Gibson, Tailor, aged 39, 23 Telford Street, bitten in the left leg.

(7) Richard Smith, aged 16, 62 Richmond Road, bitten in the left leg.

(8) John Garvey, aged 48, of 12 Franklin Street, subsequently followed me to Paris, on March 16th, under care of Mr Singer. He underwent a course of treatment similar to the other patients.

The whole of the party underwent a course of preventive treatment at Paris, each receiving one inoculation daily for ten days, as was then the regular practice.

The whole of the party which went to Paris from Bradford have continued in good health ever since.

It should be added that no charge is made for the course of treatment by Pasteur. However, the committee for administering the fund collected for the persons sent from Bradford to Paris, presented £25 to the funds of the Institut Pasteur, as a mark of gratitude for the service he had rendered to our towns-people, and for the furtherance of the scientific enquiries carried out there.

How long did it take the disease to kill poor Tom Ashworth?

Why do you think there was a delay in examining the dog?

Louis Pasteur (on the left) watching a boy being inoculated against rabies

Did the medical officer think at first that the patients would get better?

How many patients went to Paris?

Did they have to pay Pasteur for treatment?

Why do you think this was?

Pretend you are a newspaper reporter in Bradford in 1886. With a partner write a headline and a story about what happened to the people attacked by the dog. Include pictures.

Innoculations

Louis Pasteur had made important discoveries in the fight against some diseases, including rabies. By injecting or *inoculating* people with a weak dose of the rabies virus and then following this with injections of stronger doses Pasteur found he could help people's bodies build up defences against the disease. That was how he cured the people from Bradford. This method worked with other diseases as well.

Louis Pasteur working in his laboratory

Of course it had taken a long time for people to get used to the idea of having illnesses actually planted into their bodies. This cartoon was drawn about 200 years ago. It shows people having injections of a disease called cowpox. This was like smallpox, which once killed many people or left their skin terribly scarred. A small dose of cowpox helped people build up a defence against smallpox. It gave them *immunity*. (We call the injection *vaccination* from the Latin word *vacca*, which means cow.)

What does the cartoonist say would happen? Do you think this frightened people? We believe that there is no more smallpox anywhere in the world. Vaccination has destroyed it.

Have you been immunised against any diseases? Which ones? Ask at home if you don't know. Make a class list. You may have some documents which show that you have been immunised. Perhaps you can make a class wall display.

Immunisation:
just a few moments' discomfort for years of protection

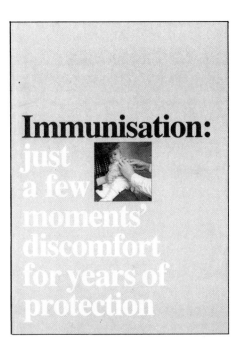

Designed by Maylin/Shaw

The usual timetable for immunisations

Age	Immunisation
From 3 months	Diphtheria Whooping cough Tetanus Polio
5-6 months	Diphtheria Whooping cough Tetanus Polio
9-11 months	Diphtheria Whooping cough Tetanus Polio
12-24 months	Measles
About 5 years	Diphtheria (booster) Tetanus (booster) Polio (booster)
Girls of ages 10 to 14	Rubella (German measles)
Girls and boys at about 13 years	Tuberculosis
15-19 years (leaving school)	Tetanus Polio

This timetable can vary. You can talk to your doctor or health visitor about immunisation against all these diseases.

And while you're thinking about your child's immunisation, it's worth asking your doctor to check whether you are immune to rubella (German measles) – to protect your next child.

HEALTH EDUCATION COUNCIL
78 New Oxford Street London WC1A 1AH

Printed by Brandprint 10/83

ID6

Five dangerous diseases

Whooping cough, diphtheria, tetanus, poliomyelitis and measles are all serious diseases. Fortunately they can all be prevented. Immunisation has helped to protect children against them and because of this none of the diseases are as common as they used to be. So it's easy for us to forget just how serious they are.

But if a child who is not protected by immunisation catches one of them, it can mean a dangerous illness. It can mean a frightening experience for the child, and a worrying and exhausting one for the parents. At worst, it can mean permanent damage to the child's health – or even death.

Whooping cough is a very common and very infectious disease. It is caught from other children who have it. It causes long and distressing bouts of coughing. These bouts can go on so long that a child finds it difficult to breathe and becomes exhausted. The coughing often ends with the child being sick and, because food isn't being kept down, the child often loses weight.

Whooping cough can also cause convulsions, hernias, ear infections, pneumonia, bronchitis and collapsed lungs. In some cases it can cause brain damage. In the ten years up to 1984, 82 children died from whooping cough in the UK.

Diphtheria begins just like a sore throat but quickly develops into a serious illness which can last for weeks. It blocks the nose or throat, making it difficult and sometimes impossible for the child to breathe. It also produces a poison which gets into the child's bloodstream and attacks the heart and nervous system. Diphtheria is now very rare in Britain, but it is still a disease that can kill.

Tetanus is caught when germs from the soil get into an open wound. It produces a poison which attacks the nervous system, causing painful muscle spasms. These spasms can happen in any muscle in the body but often they are in the jaw and neck, which is why tetanus used to be called 'lockjaw.' Tetanus is rare, but there's still a real chance of getting it and it can be fatal.

Poliomyelitis, usually called polio, now only occurs occasionally, but it's still a real risk. It attacks the nervous system and this can cause paralysis of the muscles. It can affect any muscle in the body. If it affects the breathing muscles, a child may have to be helped to breathe artificially, and even then may die. If it affects the legs, they can become weak or even paralysed, and sometimes this is permanent.

Measles is a very common disease and is highly infectious. It begins with the signs of a bad cold. Then the child gets a fever and a rash. Red spots appear behind the ears and later spread to the face and the rest of the body. The child always feels very miserable. Measles is not the trivial illness some people think it is. It can be dangerous. In fact, of all childhood infections it is the most likely to cause encephalitis (inflammation of the brain) and in a few cases this may even cause lasting brain damage. Measles can also cause ear infections and convulsions. And it can cause bronchitis and pneumonia which can sometimes lead to long-term lung troubles. About 20 children die each year from measles.

How to protect your child

Immunisation protects children against these diseases. It protects most children completely. Very rarely an immunised child does catch one of the diseases, but it is then usually very much milder and far less dangerous than if the child had not been immunised.

Immunisation against whooping cough, diphtheria, polio and measles not only protects the child who is immunised. It will also reduce risk within your family later, if you have another child. A new baby is always at risk from germs carried by older children. If the older children are immunised, then the baby is less at risk.

The vaccines which immunise against whooping cough, diphtheria and tetanus are usually combined into one 'triple' vaccine which is given by injection. Polio vaccine is given by mouth, usually at the same time as the 'triple' vaccine. Measles vaccine is given by one injection, usually slightly later.

Immunisation is quick, simple and effective. It is also free. You can read more about how it is given later in this booklet.

Leaflets explaining the benefits of inoculating children

Rabies is still a very dangerous disease as you can see by this recent newspaper report. At the moment there are no rabid animals in Britain, but other countries do have them. People are sometimes advised to have inoculations against rabies before going abroad.

This is part of a leaflet for travellers.

What is the first thing to do if you think you have been bitten by an infected animal?

Because there is no rabies in Britain, people bringing animals from other countries have to put them into *quarantine*. That means keeping them separate from other animals for some time to see if they develop the disease.

Sometimes people cheat and try to smuggle animals into Britain. Do you think this is fair? Should they be punished? How?

Look at a map of the world. If other countries have rabies, why hasn't Great Britain?

Why do you think there was a rabid dog in Bradford in 1886? What has happened between then and now?

Rabies tests for boy, 8

Tests were made yesterday on an eight-year-old boy showing symptoms of rabies. Indeppal Singh Hayre is under sedation at East Birmingham Hospital after being badly bitten by a dog while on holiday with his family in India at Christmas.

Samples from Indeppal, of Gibson Road, Handsworth, are now being tested by the Public Health Laboratory service at Colindale.

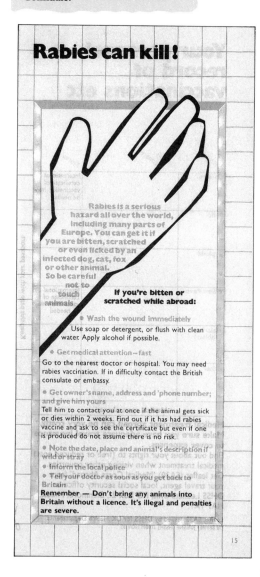

Rabies can kill!

Rabies is a serious hazard all over the world, including many parts of Europe. You can get it if you are bitten, scratched or even licked by an infected dog, cat, fox or other animal. So be careful not to touch animals.

If you're bitten or scratched while abroad:

● Wash the wound immediately
Use soap or detergent, or flush with clean water. Apply alcohol if possible.

● Get medical attention – fast
Go to the nearest doctor or hospital. You may need rabies vaccination. If in difficulty contact the British consulate or embassy.

● Get owner's name, address and 'phone number; and give him yours
Tell him to contact you at once if the animal gets sick or dies within 2 weeks. Find out if it has had rabies vaccine and ask to see the certificate but even if one is produced do not assume there is no risk.

● Note the date, place and animal's description if wild or stray

● Inform the local police

● Tell your doctor as soon as you get back to Britain

Remember — Don't bring any animals into Britain without a licence. It's illegal and penalties are severe.

15

The big clean-up

Today our streets may have litter blowing in them but they are really quite clean when compared with streets as they used to be, particularly in big towns.

Many streets had no pavements and the roads themselves were often made of earth with no tarmac or concrete. In many of the back streets, courts and alleyways there were piles of human sewage waiting for collection by local farmers. In the winter there was water and mud everywhere. Added to all this was a nuisance we do not think of today — piles of animal droppings.

In the days before cars and buses every town and city had hundreds of horses to pull wagons, carts and carriages. The back streets of the towns were full of pigsties, and sheep and cattle were often driven through the towns to the slaughter houses. All these animals left their droppings in the roadways. The smell on a hot day was terrible. In the winter many streets were covered in a thick slush of churned-up mud and sewage.

Street conditions in the 1850s

In 1886 the medical officer in Halifax wrote:

> Another matter I consider of great importance is the prompt removal of horse droppings from our main streets ... During the heat of the summer the awful smell becomes intolerable [unbearable] ... in dry weather the dust which blows into the shops is made up chiefly of this dung.

By the end of the nineteenth century most town streets were being regularly swept and cleaned. This is a report for Halifax in 1889 showing the work done:

STREETS SCAVENGING.

	1889.	1888.
Number of Streets swept	27149	25901
Area in yards	37996618	34300152
Number of Streets watered	8620	4157
Loads of water used for that purpose	12442	6255
„ Sweepings gathered	4574	4609
„ Snow removed from the Streets	972	8031
Number of Gullies emptied	89852	76661
„ Street drains flushed	306	789

What had been removed from the streets?

What are gullies?

Why do you think it was important for the drains to be flushed?

Street cleaning was just one part of the big clean-up. But it was a long time before many poor people had decent lavatories. Huge, stinking cesspits had to be drained. Middens, or earth closets, which had to be shovelled out when full, were very slowly replaced by pails or pans which could be emptied by special collectors.

The picture opposite, published in 1874, shows a dry ash toilet, which was thought to be a big improvement. Sewage was mixed with cinders and ash from the fire. At first only richer people had toilets flushed by water. These were called water closets.

Mr Netten Radcliffe Report.

PLATE XIX.

Nº 2.

MANCHESTER CORPORATION.

DRY ASH CLOSET - SECTION.

YARD

1. Excrement Pail

Slowly the pails and ash closets were changed for flushing toilets. Drains were laid under the streets and huge new reservoirs were built to supply drinking water and to work the new flushing toilets.

A reservoir in Wales built in the 1880s to supply clean water for Liverpool

Food and drink

Slowly, more people understood the importance of good food. Medical officers began to test and inspect the food coming from slaughter houses and sold in shops. They searched for meat coming from animals suffering from disease or meat that was being sold when it was bad.

Medical officers began the inspection of factories making food. One officer in London reported finding cotton fibre, bedbugs, bugs' legs, lice, fleas, bits of straw, human hair, cats' and dogs' hairs in some ice cream he tested. What must the place have been like where it was made?

You have read how dairymen sometimes poured chalk and water into their milk. Adding such things to food or drink is called *adulteration*. Often it was very serious. Children's sweets were often coloured with lead or copper which could cause sickness. Beer was adulterated with drugs and poisons which made people drunk very quickly and gave them strange, exciting dreams. This is a cartoon from the magazine, *Punch* in 1885.

Little girl: Mother says will you let her have a quarter of a pound of your best tea to kill the rats with and an ounce of chocolate ... [to] get rid of the black beetles!

This may seem funny, but adulteration of food could kill, and *Punch* was really warning people.

In 1890 this appeared in the Halifax medical officer's report:

> 114 samples of food and drugs have been analysed, of which 95 have turned out genuine, 6 of doubtful genuineness, and 13 have been adulterated. The 6 doubtful samples were milk, which were mainly marked by their poorness in cream; in 4 cases the quantity of cream was below the standard, but not sufficiently below to warrant a prosecution. The adulterated samples consisted of 2 butters, which proved to be margarine, 2 milks from which 11 and 25 per cent. of the cream had been abstracted.
>
> There has only been one prosecution during the year. A milk seller was fined £1 7s 6d., including costs, for selling milk containing 11% added water.

Today there are many regulations which people have to follow when they sell or prepare food and drink. But we are still worried about things which are being added as you can see by this recent newspaper report.

Food colourings to be curbed in new laws

NEW RESTRICTIONS on the use of colourings in food are to be introduced by the Government in the wake of widespread public concern over the effects of additives.

Mr Michael Jopling, Food and Agriculture Minister, announced that he is to prepare legislation adopting three recommendations made by the Food Advisory Committee in a report on colouring in food published yesterday.

A general wish

Prof Frank Curtis, chairman of the Food Advisory Committee said: 'We have recognised that food colours are probably the most controversial class of food additives, but appearance, and especially colour, does play an important part in our enjoyment of food.'

He said the recommendations, if adopted in full, would lead to substantial reductions in the amounts of colourings in foods, particularly drinks such as stouts and colas, biscuits and confectionery.

While there was no evidence of danger to people who consumed food colourings he said there was a general wish for them to be reduced.

Chemicals are sometimes put into food and drink to make it colourful or taste better or last longer. Food makers have to label their tins and packets with 'E' numbers to show things have been added. They also have to put a 'Sell by' date. Why?

Make a collection of food and drink wrappers, labels and tins. Include crisps, sweets, frozen foods and cereals. Are 'E' numbers printed on them? Decide whether the food and drinks they came from are good for you. You could ask your local Health Education Centre or Promotion Office to help you with this. They should have leaflets and posters which you can include in a display. The library will tell you where it is, or you could look it up in the telephone directory.

Doing it yourself

If you want to find old medical officers' reports like the ones I have put in this book, ask about them at your local library. The librarians will help you. The language is sometimes hard to understand so you will need a dictionary.

If you have read *Thanks for the Memory* in this series you will know what *oral history* means. Talk·to some older people about the things you have read about in this book. You should be able to collect a lot more evidence like this. For example, I have not written much about bathing or washing clothes in the past. What about the sorts of medicines people used to take? What were hospitals like?

Here is what one old lady said about what used to happen when she was young.

Our nessy (lavatory) was at the end of the garden. We shared it with another family. It had a seat with a hole. I thought it was marvellous to go to Huddersfield to my auntie's because she had a bathroom.

A nessy

They fetched people to the fever hospital when they had scarlet fever. A cart came pulled by horses. They had to stay in hospital for seven weeks until their skin stopped peeling. You couldn't go near the cart. It was blue or black with dark windows so you couldn't see in. We didn't go near in case we caught the fever.

INDEX

ACKNOWLEDGEMENTS

The author and publishers would like to thank the following for permission to reproduce material:

BBC Hulton Picture Library **pp 12, 32, 33, 39**; British Museum **p 54**; Department of Education and Science **p 4**; Daily Telegraph **pp 30, 56, 61**; Mary Evans Picture Library **pp 24, 28, 31**; Greater London Council **pp 8, 10**; Guildhall Library **p 41**; House of Lords Record Office Parliamentary paper on Public Health, Supplementary Report to the Local Government Board, Appendix 7, Plate XIX, 1874, xxxi **P 59** (top); Liverpool City Libraries **p 59** (bottom); By permission of the Master and Fellows of Magdalene College, Cambridge **pp 17, 19** (bottom); Mansell Collection **pp 26** (top), **27, 37, 38, 53, 57**; Museum of London **p19** (top); National Society for the Prevention of Cruelty to Children **p 9**; Punch Publications **pp 36, 47, 60**; Ann Ronan Picture Library **p 52**; The Times, 22 May 1987, report by Mark Ellis, photo by John Rogers **p 13**; Tolson Memorial Museum, West Kirklees **p 11**; Richard Worsnop **p 26** (bottom)

Artwork by children at Wooldale Junior School, Kirklees, West Yorkshire **pp 20, 29**

Artwork by John Booth **pp 24, 43**

Cover design by David Armitage

Designed by Bob Wright